10 DOs
& DON'Ts
when you're the
NEW KID

10 DOs & DON'Ts

when you're the

NEW KID

*A survival guide for teens
starting at a new school*

J.C. TILTON

TWO HARBORS PRESS

Two Harbors Press
212 3rd Avenue North, Suite 290
Minneapolis, MN 55401
612.455.2293
www.TwoHarborsPress.com

ISBN-13: 978-1-937293-93-2
LCCN: 2011942881

Distributed by Itasca Books

Book Design by Kristeen Ott
Illustrations by Mara Shaughnessy

Printed in the United States of America

To my parents,

without whose love, hard work, and willingness

to relocate for better opportunities,

my book would be titled:

10 Dos & Don'ts

When You Live in One Boring Place Your Entire Life

CONTENTS

INTRODUCTION

So, you're moving. Maybe you've lived most of your life in the same city or even the same house. Or maybe this is the third time you've been uprooted since the *Twilight* saga hit theaters. Whatever your situation, moving to a new school is tough. In elementary school, barring any unfortunate pants-wetting incidents, you could usually find a new best friend by the end of the first day. In junior high it got harder, especially for girls. In high school . . . well, let's just say you'll have plenty of material for a book one day.

Of course, moving has its advantages too. It can be a great opportunity to reinvent yourself. At your new school, no one remembers when you barfed at the freshman dance or missed the game-deciding free throw when your basketball team went to state. You're an unknown quantity. All your fellow students know is what they observe and what you tell them. That's why your first days at a new school are so important. You've no doubt heard the expression "You never get a second chance to make a first impression." This is one of the truest of all truisms. So take control where you can from day one. With a little planning, confidence, and a sense of humor, you can avoid common pitfalls and make your move a bit smoother.

My Story

I moved a lot growing up, and this is the book I wish someone had given me. Frankly, the "just be yourself and everyone will like you" advice from my parents wasn't much comfort as I walked around the lunchroom, desperately seeking a place to sit. I hope you can benefit from my experience, or at least have a good laugh.

I attended three elementary schools, two junior highs, and three high schools. Although the earlier moves are a blur, I remember clearly the move from Iowa to Minnesota in ninth grade. If you live in the United States, you probably know that Iowa, as a state, enjoys a unique level of disdain. Synonymous with a lack of sophistication, it is openly mocked by people from all the other states—even North Dakota. To make matters worse, there's a long-running rivalry between Minnesota and Iowa, which I believe is rooted in college football, but over the years has expanded to include pretty much all other facets of life in either state.

During my first week at school, I was asked about a thousand times if I knew what IOWA stood for. For those of you not from the Midwest, it's "Idiots Out Wandering Around." People wanted to know if we'd lived in a cornfield. Had I ever been to a mall before, or did we buy everything from mail-order catalogs? (Mind you, this snobbery was coming from ninth-graders in Burnsville, Minnesota. It's not like I'd transferred to the Sorbonne. I think it's a safe bet that most Parisians would be snickering at the people who were snickering at me.)

I listened to a lot of stupid comments and tried to laugh. My younger sister had a better strategy. She told everyone we were from St. Louis.

I made more than a few mistakes during this particular move. First, I totally overdressed—dresses, pantyhose, and high heels—every day. I thought I looked sophisticated and "big city." (Okay, maybe I was kind of a hick.) Teachers loved me. Popular girls tried to trip me. I'm not suggesting that you become a clone and suit up in Abercrombie & Fitch forever; I'm just saying that the first weeks at school will be easier if you're not trying to make fashion history. That brings me to mistake number two: clique-hopping. I started by hanging out with the nerdy but nice kids, the only ones who made any effort to welcome me. I repaid their kindness by moving on to the semi-popular kids, with whom I actually had a lot in common. Then, through sheer determination, I made it into the popular group and that nirvana of popular girls—cheerleading.

Sadly, it was not to last. I was bored to death with both cheerleading and that group of kids in general. Soon, I started hanging out in downtown Minneapolis and got into punk rock. I sported a mohawk—perhaps my most unflattering hairstyle ever. I wore nothing but black. (I still do, but now it's for the slimming effect.) This instigated my immediate descent from the in-crowd. You know you're no longer popular when the guys you used to cheer for at football games start throwing gum at you. Chewed gum. Of course, the semi-popular kids, who liked the same bands and clothes as I did, weren't too friendly anymore either, as I'd pretty much dumped them when I made cheerleading. Fortunately, I guess, I didn't have to live with the situation too long, because in my junior year we moved to Grand Rapids, Michigan. But that's a whole other story.

#1

DO

what you (and your parents) can
to make your first day easier

Be prepared.

Motto of the Boy Scouts of America

Your parents are not moving because they want to make your life miserable. There's probably a very good reason for the move—a new job, a home that works better for your family . . . or maybe the Feds are closing in. *Why* isn't important. What is important is that your parents are almost certainly worried about you and are willing to do almost anything to help ease the transition. This is a good time to hit them up for a new car. (Just kidding. Well, mostly kidding.) The good news is that there are specific things you and your parents can do to help take a little stress out of your first day at your new school. It's your job to make a plan and let your parents know how they can help.

5 Simple Steps to a Better First Day

1. **Make a practice run.** Performers hold dress rehearsals. Emergency workers run disaster drills. That's because actually going through the actions of any task is different from just knowing intellectually

3

what to do. For example, on an academic level I totally understand how to do CPR—but I'd hate to have someone's life depend on my memory of the Red Cross class I took six years ago.

Ask your parents to help you get your schedule and locker number a day or two before you start. Visit the school and walk the route to your classes. Try out your locker combination. Hang a few pictures, if you'd like. Find out where the bathrooms, lunchroom, library, and gym are located. It's a lot easier to get oriented when you're not under first-day stress, rushing between classes.

2. **Meet the neighbors.** Unless you've moved into a retirement community, there are probably lots of kids in your new neighborhood who go to your new school. If possible, spend some time outside so it's easy for neighbor kids to meet you. They probably won't ring your doorbell and introduce themselves, but if you're out shooting hoops it's a lot easier to say hi. Your parents can also make a point of introducing themselves to the neighbors sooner rather than later, and very likely your neighbors will volunteer their son or daughter to show you around on your first day. Whether you want to accept this help is up to you, but it's nice to have a friendly face on the bus or in the hall on the first day.

3. **Take advantage of help, if offered.** Few schools have programs specifically to help new students, but if you (or your parents) don't ask, you'll never know. Some schools have student volunteers looking for ways to help the school/ingratiate themselves with the faculty. (At college they will be the ones giving campus tours to prospective students—probably a college that accepted them based on letters of recommendation from the aforementioned high school faculty.) Whatever their motivation, it's a big plus to have a student show you around on your first day. You might have nothing in common with this person, or it might be the beginning of a beautiful friendship, a la Napoleon Dynamite and Pedro. At the very least, you won't get lost.

4. **Know your intro.** Most teachers announce new students to the class. Everyone will turn to look at you. This is where you smile casually, like you've done this a hundred times before. Some teachers won't say anything at all, but believe me, somewhere in your near future there will be a well-meaning educator who will say, "Why don't you tell the class a little bit about yourself?" This teacher has completely forgotten what it's like to be a teenager, a time when no one wants to stand up in front of a bunch of strangers and talk about herself. It is ever so much better to know what you're going to say ahead of time. (When you're put on the spot, details like your name and

hometown tend to slip your mind.) Your introduction should be simple, something like "I'm _____. We just moved here from _____." Please note that this is usually a bad time to try out a new joke or that hilarious accent you've been working on.

5. **Have a Plan B for lunch.** Lunch is the hardest time of day when you're new. It's the one period without any seating assignment or real structure. In theory, any student can sit anywhere in the cafeteria. In practice, it's never that simple. If you're the super-confident type, by all means approach a table and plant yourself. At sixteen, I was not the super-confident type, and one of my least favorite memories is of asking kids if I could join them at a lunch table and getting their unenthusiastic response. In general, you want to avoid asking fellow students for permission in social situations.

Instead, consider bringing something easy to eat the first few days, like a granola bar and fruit, so you can eat fairly quickly in the lunchroom or anywhere else. Getting to the cafeteria a few minutes early is a good idea too. When you're already seated, people will be joining your table, which is a completely different dynamic. When kids sit down at your table, be sure to smile and be friendly. Don't try to insert yourself into their conversation unnaturally, but if they seem open to it, introduce yourself. You can also ask a question about where your next class is located (even if you know the answer). People generally like to feel helpful. Keep in mind, these suggestions are just for the first few days, not something you should do forever. By your second week at your new school, you'll wonder why you were ever worried about it.

Parents Just Don't Understand . . . and Here's Why

Your parents may not understand why going to a new school is such a big deal. If they didn't move when they were younger, they have no firsthand experience to draw upon. Adults generally think of moving as a great opportunity to meet new people and expand your horizons. This is because being new in town as an adult is a whole different gig from being the "new kid." When they're new to a job, people shake their hand and invite them to lunch. When they're new in the neighborhood, people shake their hand and give them muffins. There's a known and accepted structure for how adults interact. Parents don't realize that when you walk into the lunchroom alone on your first day, no one is going to call out, "Laura, please join us! We're discussing the World History syllabus."

#2

DON'T

be a drowning swimmer

Help! I have nothing to do Friday night!

Desperation is like stealing from the mafia. You have a
good chance of attracting the wrong attention.
Doug Horton

Everyone loves a metaphor. At least, all my English
teachers did. That's why I'm starting this chapter with a
metaphorical drowning swimmer. Nothing sends people
running in the opposite direction faster than desperation.
This is a cardinal rule throughout life, whether you're
interviewing for a job, dating, or anything else. The
expression "never let them see you sweat" sounds trite,
but it's first-rate advice. (Perhaps the only first-rate advice
to come from a 1984 deodorant commercial.) Keeping a
cool and calm demeanor, when you're flailing inside, is a
useful skill. Of course when you move to a new school,
it's natural to feel a bit lost. The point is that no one at your
new school has to know you're flailing inside. There's no
reason to keep your feelings bottled up, but share your
frustrations with your family and old friends who already
know and love you, not with your new classmates.

Make an Effort—Just Don't Overdo It

Working hard is a virtue when it comes to things like academics or training for the Olympics. When it comes to making friends, not so much. When you meet people with whom you have a genuine connection or at least common interests, there's no need to put on a front. You feel comfortable just being yourself and conversation comes naturally. Conversely, actively trying to fit in with a group usually has the opposite of the intended effect. You may come across as disingenuous, looking like a poser, and make others uncomfortable. For a super-creepy version of this behavior, see *The Talented Mr. Ripley* with Matt Damon—that's trying too hard to a psychopathic degree!

You should absolutely be open and enthusiastic about building new friendships, but remember that people with their own passions and interests tend to attract others—while someone whose only interest is in getting people to like him or her is less likely to be seen as a desirable friend. You don't have to play hard to get, but being overly available or submissive isn't a good strategy either. Go for the happy medium. Remember, it's human nature to want what you haven't got and to value relationships less when they come too easily. For classic cinematic (but not super-creepy) examples, see any John Hughes movie from the 1980s—*Pretty in Pink*, *Sixteen Candles*, or *Some Kind of Wonderful*.

The Big No-No: Can I Come Along?

A sure way to seem desperate is to invite yourself to anything. It puts the other person on the spot, and nobody wants to feel like a jerk, so he'll say, "Sure, come along," whether he really wants you to or not. Now you have the perfect beginning to an awkward outing. Of course, being new means you have to take initiative to make one-on-one plans; just do it the right way. Wait long enough to find out which person (or people) you actually might like, and then ask that person to do something—like going to a movie or other activity that doesn't put a lot of pressure on keeping up constant conversation. If your invitee says no, don't keep asking. Say "Maybe some other time," and then leave it up to that person to ask you.

#3

DO

join the team, club, or band

Eighty percent of success is showing up.
Woody Allen

One of the hardest things about being new is feeling like you need an invitation—essentially, someone's permission—to participate. With teams or school-sponsored clubs, this isn't the case. You're as entitled as anyone else to join in. Personally, I haven't liked group activities since my first Girl Scout meeting. So why am I telling you to suit-up for something? Because, quite simply, it will make your transition easier. Organized activities get you out of the house and interacting with new people in a somewhat structured way. You don't have to commit to lifelong membership, just give something a try. Not only will you meet more people more quickly, but participating in school and community organizations helps to beef up your college applications. (I had a hard time turning a single semester of lackluster cheerleading into an extracurricular activity section that would impress any admissions committee.)

The ABCs of Extracurricular Activities

In addition to getting you out and about, being part of a formal group offers a ton of benefits.

Automatic Conversation Starter

It can be intimidating even for adults to walk up and introduce themselves to new people. In the halls of the average high school, it's simply not done. When you participate in the same activity with a person, however, there's a legitimate reason to communicate. Even if the only thing you say is "What time is practice?" or "Great game," it breaks the ice in a way that's natural for both of you. Bonus: the adult in charge—your coach, bandleader, or teacher—will introduce you to the group when you join, which is a lot quicker than meeting one person at a time.

Better Busy Than Bummed Out

Moving is stressful, and it can be depressing, and there's nothing depression loves more than an evening at home, wallowing in self-pity and pizza. (I gained about ten pounds every time we moved. It wasn't good.) Action—any kind of activity, really—is a fantastic remedy for depression. It's next to impossible to maintain a sense of isolation and sadness while you rip around the soccer field or bust out a tune on the tuba. Plus, if you're part of an organized group, it's not up to you alone to summon the motivation to get out and be active every day. Your team is counting on you to show up and most times, that's all the push you need.

Colleges Look for Balance

Most college admission boards are interested in more than test scores and grades. Participating in organized activities—whether school-, community-, or work-related—shows prospective schools and employers that you are able to manage your time and responsibilities and that you honor your commitments. Of course, it's more impressive to be an officer or leader in an organization and to be involved for more than a semester here or there.

#4

DON'T

freak out about

hanging solo for a while

> Friendship with one's self is all-important,
> because without it one cannot be friends
> with anyone else in the world.
>
> *Eleanor Roosevelt*

When you're new, about a month of relative solitude comes with the territory. Expect it. Deal with it. Embrace it—or at least don't freak out about it. Lots of people are uncomfortable being by themselves, imagining that everyone else is at a fabulous party, having the time of their lives. Try to remember that not having plans for the first few weekends doesn't mean you're unloved, unpopular, or neglected. It means that you're new, and no one has had a chance to get to know you yet. Also, you're unlikely to die of boredom since you have video games, the Internet, and two thousand TV channels to help you pass the time. In fact, you've got more entertainment options at your fingertips than people have had at any other point in the history of the world, so make sure you don't go to the other extreme and spend endless hours inside alone every day. The lack of natural sunlight isn't healthy. (Plus, only Robert Pattinson can pull off that level of pastiness.)

You Are Who You Hang With—So Take Your Time

Don't make a habit of hanging out with kids you aren't comfortable with just to avoid another Friday night with Netflix and your parents—especially if they're doing things you don't agree with, like drinking. The best thing to do is try to meet as many different people as possible during your first weeks at school. If you start going out frequently with one group—with kids known for using drugs, for example—you'll be lumped in with them quicker than you can say, "The new kid's a stoner." Sure, it takes time to get to know a person before you can decide if you'd like to have him or her as a friend, but in your gut you know pretty quickly who might be a good fit for you. Listen to your intuition!

Help Others and Yourself at the Same Time

If you find yourself itching to get out of the house, volunteering is another great way to spend your extra time. Thousands of organizations would love to have a smart, energetic student like you. There are so many places—animal shelters, nursing homes, food pantries, hospitals, parks, art museums, libraries, community centers, and zoos, to name a few. Pick something you like, and then pick up the phone.

Why volunteer?

- It helps your fellow man (woman and child), animals, or the environment.
- It distracts you from the stress of being the new kid.
- It gets you out of the house in a constructive way.
- It provides an easy way to meet like-minded people.
- It looks great on college applications.

Not sure where to start? Check out these sites for volunteering opportunities in your area:

- www.1-800-volunteer.org
- www.volunteermatch.com
- www.dosomething.org

10 Lessons You Can Learn From High School Movies

1. *High School Musical*—Be yourself. Follow your heart. Know when to ignore your friends.
2. *Mean Girls*—Stay true to yourself and never forget your real friends.
3. *Napoleon Dynamite*—Nice guys can win in the end.
4. *Easy A*—Double standards about sex are still alive and well.
5. *An Education*—A British accent makes even the dumbest statements sound clever and insightful.
6. *Clueless*, *10 Things I Hate About You*, and *O*—Shakespeare still puts butts in seats.
7. *Ferris Bueller's Day Off*—Don't forget to stop and smell the roses once in a while.
8. *Superbad*—Being really funny overcomes being pretty homely . . . if you're a guy.
9. *Twilight* saga—Vampires are just better kissers.
10. *Juno*—Sarcasm and wit may help take the sting out of being a pregnant teen, but it still sucks.

#5

DON'T

take any crap

Courage is fire, and bullying is smoke.
Benjamin Disraeli

My grandfather moved around a lot as a boy. His parents were farmers during the Great Depression, and each time they moved he had to fight the toughest kid in school to establish his place in the pecking order. Thankfully, times have changed considerably since then, but the principle still applies: it's important to stand up for yourself from day one. As an esteemed philosopher (or maybe it was Dr. Phil) once said: in life, we teach people how to treat us. If you accept negative behavior, you set a precedent. If you insist upon being treated with respect and treat others that way, you establish ground rules. That's not to say you should look for confrontations to prove you're not intimidated—on the contrary, you want to enter your new school smoothly and seamlessly, like a high diver slicing into the surface of the pool. (Cannonballs and belly flops are another option, but unless you've got the charisma and comedic chops of, say, Jack Black, I don't recommend them.)

When General Jerkiness Escalates into Bullying

As you journey through life, keep in mind this universal truth: some people are just jerks. There's not much you can do—or *not* do, for that matter—to change them or get them to like you. Avoid them when possible, and if you can't avoid them, ignore them. If they make themselves un-ignorable, you have to take action—and the sooner the better. Bullies need to know up front you won't tolerate being treated badly. Let them get away with it once, and you can be sure it will happen again.

10 Tips for Dealing with Bullies—Online and at School

1. **Tell your parents and the school right away.** It's way better to have a bully call you a tattletale and leave you alone than to endure weeks of stress and misery.

2. **Try not to feel ashamed or embarrassed by the bully's behavior.** It's not your fault he or she is picking on you. Because you're new, the bully may be testing the waters to see what you'll do—that's why standing up for yourself from day one is so important.

3. **Do your best not to react to taunts.** Bullies thrive on getting a rise out of their target. This doesn't mean allowing someone to treat you badly, simply that it takes the excitement out of picking on you if you don't respond or seem to care.

4. **Make a note of the times and places each incident occurs.** If the harassment escalates, your documentation can help the school in punishing or expelling the bullying student.

5. **If a bully physically harms you, go to an adult immediately.** This is assault and needs to be dealt with as the serious issue that it is.

6. **Try to walk with a friend, teacher, or classmate between classes.** Bullies tend to be pretty cowardly when they're outnumbered.

7. **Use technology to your advantage.** Print copies of posts, IMs, and e-mails that contain nasty or threatening language. You may even be able to capture the bullying behavior on your cell phone. That way, it's not your word against the bully's. (Plus, it gives most people pause when they realize their bad behavior is being recorded.)

8. **Report online harassment to the website on which it occurs.** Most social websites have policies to protect members from online abuse and harassment. On Facebook, for example, it's simple to report a message, page, individual, or group. For more information, visit the website's Help Center and search for "Reporting a violation."

9. **Manage your online persona.** Be sure to set your privacy preferences so that only people you've approved can access your page. Block IMs and e-mails from anyone you don't want to hear from. You wouldn't stay on the phone listening to someone insult you—treat the Internet the same way.

10. **Find out if your new school has an anti-bullying policy—and don't be afraid to use it.** Tell a teacher, counselor, or coach you're being bullied. If that person isn't able to help you, tell another adult. Many schools even have harassment/bullying report forms you can download online. Once you've made an official complaint, the school has to take action or face the consequences.

Taking legal action— is it overreacting?

Imagine your father (or any adult) just started a new job. He's walking down the hallway one day when suddenly Larry, from accounting, shoves him into the wall and calls him a loser. Maybe Larry hates the way your dad does spreadsheets. Whatever. What do you think your dad would do? Would he sulk away, feeling bad about himself? Avoid the men's room and cafeteria because Larry might be there? Doubtful. In the adult world, human resources, lawyers, and probably the police would be involved right away. Charges would be filed. Larry would be fired. The situation would be resolved.

When a person physically harms you **or even threatens to do so,** you are protected by law. If your school won't or can't take care of the problem, you and your parents should consider consulting a lawyer. A letter from an attorney can work wonders with the school and the bully's parents.

#6

DO
know your audience

Tact is the ability to describe others
as they see themselves.
Eleanor Chaffee

Anyone who's done a lot of public speaking or performing will tell you, nothing is more important than knowing your audience. Let's say you were asked to give a speech on dinosaurs at the local library. You know a ton about all things prehistoric, and you prepare an awesome speech with the latest theories about extinction and the evolution of dinosaurs to birds. When you arrive for your talk, you notice that the average age of the audience is four. You get questions like, "Which dinosaur made the biggest poop?" and "Who would win if a T rex fought Spiderman?" You realize your material is not going to work with this group, and you're supposed to keep their attention for forty-five minutes. It's a lesson you can apply to almost any situation.

How can you know your audience—the other kids at school—when you're the new kid? Of course you can't know everything, but you can make a few educated assumptions. It's a good bet your new classmates don't see themselves as hicks or morons. (Not even hicks and morons see themselves that way.) You can also assume that your being open, interested, and sincere is a good way to start. Learn something about the town and the school before you move. You don't have to do a history report, just get a feel for the city. Check out the school's website. Familiarize yourself with the major local attractions, sports teams, and events, and then try not to insult them. For example, if you moved to Green Bay, Wisconsin, wearing a T-shirt that reads, "Bratwurst sucks!" or "I hate football!" would be a mistake. You might very well hate sausages and sports, and that's perfectly fine, but there's no reason it should be the first thing your new classmates learn about you as you stroll through the halls.

Big city to small town: If you move from a bigger city to a smaller town, people will have preconceptions about you. They'll be interested in you—but they probably won't want to *seem* interested in you. No matter how hard it is, try not to show any attitude about how much smaller/ inferior you think your new town is. Make positive comments, like "It's so cool that you can ride your bike everywhere," even if you don't mean it. Being tactful is a great skill to have throughout life. Plus, this will prepare you for adulthood when you have to say things like, "Of course, I'd love to do a demanding internship for no pay!"

Small town to big city: If you move from a small town to a bigger city, people may have a preconception of you as a hick but probably nothing more specific. For example, when you imagine a person from Manhattan, certain stereotypes come to mind—maybe an impatient, black-clad person who talks fast and thinks New York is the only real city in the country. Now think of a person from Kearney, Nebraska. Not so many stereotypes on that one. Tell people what you like about your new city without going overboard. Comments along the lines of "It's cool to be in a place with more than one movie theater" will play better than staring open-mouthed at buildings, saying, "Wow, we didn't have any skyscrapers in my old town."

Another Real Life Lesson: If You Can't Say Anything nice . . .

When I was in fifth grade we moved from Des Moines, Iowa, to Storm Lake, a very small town in the northwest part of the state. As we drove around Storm Lake, I made several nasty comments about the town. I was mad about having to move. (And in my defense, they didn't even have a mall.) Later we stopped by the local bank so my parents could finish some paperwork. The banker welcomed us and introduced us to a few of his co-workers. At that point my younger sister, then seven years old, announced loudly, "My sister says this town is a real sewer." The loan officer smiled politely. My parents looked mortified. Even I had the good sense to be embarrassed. No one wants to feel looked down upon. Even people who hate where they live and can't wait to leave are defensive when a newcomer insults their home turf. It's kind of like with families—I can make fun of my mom, but you can't.

The 10 Worst Answers to the Question, "So, Where Are You From?"

We're all from *somewhere*. But saying you just moved to town from Spokane, Washington, probably isn't going to raise eyebrows. The names on this list, on the other hand, are likely to get some laughs. (This is where being able to laugh at yourself comes in handy.) These are legitimate names of real American towns. Most of them have a chamber of commerce that would be glad to send you information on their community. Go ahead—look them up!

1. Hell, Michigan (*okay, this could actually be kind of cool*)
2. Looneyville, Texas
3. Fleatown, Ohio
4. Intercourse, Pennsylvania
5. Virginville, Pennsylvania
6. Blue Ball, Pennsylvania (*Anyone else starting to think Pennsylvania may have some issues?*)
7. Boogertown, North Carolina
8. Boring, Oregon
9. Spread Eagle, Wisconsin
10. Maggie's Nipple, Wyoming

#7

DON'T
over-share

Whoever gossips to you will gossip about you.
Spanish proverb

In general, guys bond through shared experiences like sports and combat, or through playing video games involving sports and combat. Girls tend to bond by sharing confidences, and often they share too much information too soon. Wait until you know and trust a person before you reveal your innermost thoughts and secrets. It's not that you should be ashamed of who you are or how you feel, merely that people need a chance to get to know you first, and that takes time. What if the first time Edward met Bella, he said, "Hi, I'm a vampire, but don't worry—I only suck the blood of animals." That's simply TMI way too soon.

Share—Don't Bare

Real friendships take time to develop, like fine wine or smelly cheese. Don't try to rush things by over-disclosing. There's a huge difference between sharing interesting tidbits about yourself and indiscriminatingly blabbing your most personal information. A few examples:

Sharing: "My family took our first skiing trip last year, and I had a huge crush on the instructor."

Baring: "I have recurring bladder infections that necessitate the use of adult diapers."

Sharing: "When I gave a speech at my old school, I was so nervous that I literally couldn't speak."

Baring: "At my old school, everyone called me the Peeper."

Be wary of people who ask overly personal questions before you've taken them into your confidence—that's a red flag for someone without good boundaries. There's a difference between appropriate interest (e.g., "Why did your family move here?") and inappropriate nosiness (e.g., "Why did you parents get divorced?" or "Are you a virgin?"). Don't feel like you have to answer every question you're asked. A good strategy for deflecting uncomfortable queries is to laugh them off, like, "OMG, I can't believe you asked me that!" Then change the subject to something you'd rather talk about.

Broadcasting Bad Judgment—Around the Globe and for All Eternity

Facebook, MySpace, Twitter, and a zillion other social websites are an awesome way to connect with friends and family. They're also an instantaneous way to over-share personal photos and information with more people than you intended . . . way more people. A good rule of thumb is: if you'd be embarrassed for your mom to see it, don't post it. If you're doing something illegal and ill-advised, like underage drinking, don't post it. Sure, you can limit access through passwords and privacy settings, but the bottom line is that once it's on the Web, it's out there. Pictures that are hilarious now won't be as funny when they keep you from getting a job you want or making a good impression on people you meet in the future.

It's not that other people didn't do anything crazy, stupid, or weird when they were your age. It's that they didn't show the poor judgment of posting evidence of it for the world to see and comment on. (Okay, they didn't have the option when they were your age—the technology didn't exist until the mid-'90s—but you get the idea.) Post wisely.

TIP! Don't text sexually explicit pictures or language. EVER. Today's *true love* can become tomorrow's **ex-from-hell** in a flash—almost as quickly as an embarrassing photo can be forwarded to thousands, nay millions, of people. Never forget: once you push send, that image is completely out of your control. For real-life examples, check out the daily headlines and see which politician, professional athlete, or celebrity is in damage-control mode for inappropriate texting.

#8

DO

fake it till you make it

I didn't mean to blow up the science lab, but
hey, these things happen . . .

If you think you can do a thing
or you think you can't do a thing, you're right.
Henry Ford

Self-confidence is amazingly powerful—in school, at work, in romance. Where desperation repels, confidence attracts. Confidence is sexy. Confidence, especially when combined with talent, transforms even the most unattractive person into a god among men. (For examples, see every member of the Rolling Stones.) Understandably, when you're starting at a new school you might not feel like running down the halls yelling "I'm king of the world!" That's really not a good idea for many reasons. But don't slouch around, mumbling to yourself, either. This is where you fake it to the best of your ability. It's not unlike acting. In fact, it is acting, but you may be surprised how quickly real confidence grows.

10 Tips to a More Confident You

On the outside . . .

1. **Smile.** You may notice that people on TV—from politicians to actors to CEOs—are usually smiling. The image they project is positive and confident, even when they're discussing an uncomfortable topic. Having an easy smile is an asset in life off-screen too. Don't go overboard, of course. I'm not talking a goofy, ever-present *SpongeBob SquarePants* kind of smile. More of a friendly, how-you-doing kind of smile. It helps to practice in the mirror. (Not in the restroom mirror at school . . .)

2. **Make eye contact.** The appropriate amount of eye contact is largely cultural. In some places, direct eye contact conveys something very different than simple interest or sincerity. In many Asian societies, prolonged direct eye contact is considered disrespectful, even aggressive. In American culture, looking away frequently while you're speaking can imply shiftiness. On the other hand, staring unblinkingly into a person's eyes will probably make him or her uncomfortable—unless that person is deeply in love with you . . . or insane (and hopefully not both). Try for a happy medium.

3. **Speak clearly and calmly.** Easier said than done, right? When I'm nervous, I talk incredibly fast. Others hem and haw, or use filler words such as "like" and "you know" to an annoying degree. Controlling the tempo and tone of your voice can be tough. Before speaking up in class, try taking a deep breath and sitting up straight. If you're going to give a presentation, take the time beforehand to practice. (A great speaker once told me he practiced for hours before a speech in order to sound spontaneous onstage.) You can even record yourself, or have a friend do it, to see how you actually look and sound—and unlike a mortifying "sexy" photo, it's unlikely that you practicing your speech on Shakespeare will become an Internet sensation.

4. **Give compliments with sincerity.** Obvious flattery is off-putting, but it's hard to ignore a genuine compliment. Be sure it's not too personal or just plain weird, such as, "You looked so awesome coming out of the bathroom stall." Or backhanded, such as, "Wow, those pants rock—not like the ones you wore yesterday." Try something more along the lines of "Nice catch," or "I love your shoes."

   Accept compliments with grace. When you're on the receiving end of an admiring comment, be gracious. Don't deflect a compliment about your ensemble with "Oh, this old thing. I hate it." Girls often feel compelled to do this, as if responding to a compliment with a simple thank you is equivalent to agreeing with it and therefore appearing conceited. Just say "Thanks!"

5. **Dress the part.** It's hard to feel like the proverbial million bucks when you're not totally comfortable in what you're wearing. When you look good, you feel better. It's worth it to take a little extra time on yourself in the morning. Choose your clothes the night before. Wear one of your favorite outfits, provided it's weather and school-dress-code appropriate. Girls, keep your makeup simple and clean. The key word here is understated. You want to look like you made an effort, not like you've been primping since 3:00 a.m. for a stroll down the red carpet.

On the inside . . .

6. **Know you're not alone.** No matter what people show the world, everyone feels insecure at times. In fact, the most outwardly arrogant people are often the most insecure. They cover it up by acting obnoxious. You don't have to do that. You just have to do your best. Every time you make it through a challenging situation, you'll get stronger and more self-assured. Someday you'll be able to walk into any new situation with genuine confidence—who knows, one day you might even look back on moving as invaluable experience!

7. **Remember not to take it personally.** We all care, to some degree, what other people think. No one wants to be thought of as stupid or mean or ugly, but what others think isn't in your control. Realize that throughout life you'll meet people who immediately like you, and who you like in return. You'll also meet people where the lack of chemistry between you is obvious. In these cases, minimize contact and move on.

8. **Do what you already do well.** Doing something you're already good at makes you feel more confident. Your first week at a new school isn't the ideal time to try that activity that's always intimidated you—say, stand-up comedy or ski jumping, especially not in public. Know your element and stick to it while your real inner confidence grows. There'll be plenty of time to try new things when you're a bit more settled.

9. **Focus on a goal.** Goals are positive distractions. When you're intent upon reaching an objective, you're less apt to obsess over every little thing. You can set a goal related to being the new kid, like talking to one new person every day. Or you can set a more personal goal, like calling your grandmother every week or memorizing every word of *The Lord of the Rings* trilogy. Or memorizing *LOTR* and reciting it over the phone to your grandmother. As long as it's engaging and positive, it's fine.

10. **Learn to laugh at yourself.** When you can laugh at yourself, you make it less fun for those people who might tease you. Drop your tray in the lunchroom? Take a bow. Knock over a rack of books in the library? Say, "I meant to do that." Self-deprecating humor is usually endearing, as long as it doesn't deteriorate into self-mockery.

What's the difference between self-deprecation and self-mockery? Glad you asked. Let's say you're running full speed across the gym when you trip over your own feet and totally bite it. Loudly. Now you're flat on your back with everyone staring at you. Self-deprecation would be saying, "And that's why I'm not a ballerina." Self-mockery would be saying something like, "I'm such a clumsy jerk. I shouldn't even be allowed to take gym class. Why do I even try . . ." Everyone has embarrassing moments—don't let yours get you down.

#9

DON'T

lose touch with your old life

Make new friends, but keep the old.
One is silver and the other gold.
Girl Scout song

Saying good-bye to good friends is hard, and the way you choose to mark the occasion is purely personal preference. Do you want a big blowout with everyone you know? Or is a quiet night with a few close friends more your style? You don't have to make a big emotional event out of saying good-bye, but it is important to acknowledge that the life you and your friends share is changing in a big way. It's also important to realize friendships don't die just because one person leaves town. With technology like texting, webcams, and e-mail, staying in touch is simpler than ever before—but that doesn't mean it's easy. As you make new friends and feel more comfortable at your new school, it will get more challenging to keep up the frequent e-mails and calls with old friends. The key to staying in touch is making it a priority.

5 Tips for Keeping in Touch

1. **Plan virtual visits.** You're probably already linked to your friends on Facebook, MySpace, or Twitter, but nothing replaces real-time, face-to-face (or at least monitor-to-monitor) contact. Chat live, across the miles, with easy-to-use video conferencing from Skype, Windows Live Messenger, Face Time (Mac users), and many others. All you need is a webcam—they're built into most computers and smartphones now—and a broadband connection. You can usually download the software for free, and there are no long-distance or roaming charges to deal with. I highly recommend setting a regular schedule for these, like Sunday nights after dinner. Whether it's once a week or once a month, your web chats are much more likely to occur if you plan them ahead of time.

2. **Visit in person when you can.** Life in your old town will go on without you. (It won't be as much fun, of course!) If you can, go back to visit in a few months. It's helpful to have a reunion to look forward to, and knowing you will see your buddies again soon can help take a little of the melancholy out of saying good-bye. When you go, you may be surprised by how your perspective has changed. You might find yourself appreciating things you never noticed before or being relieved that you don't have to deal with certain people or situations. Also, try not to

be jealous that your old friends have formed new relationships. No one can replace you, just like your new friends can never replace your old BFF.

3. **Remember birthdays.** Cell phone or computer alerts for birthdays and other special occasions can help you to appear wonderfully thoughtful. A quick call, text, or e-card is all it takes to let your friends know you're thinking of them. I'm a big fan of e-cards—they're instant, usually free, and now there are lots of cool ones to choose from. Check out Smilebox, Rattlebox, and Blue Mountain for a variety of inspired designs for every occasion. If you're looking for hilarious, irreverent, and generally sarcastic e-cards check out WrongCards or someecards.

4. **Think beyond the weekend get-together.** With a little planning you could spend an entire summer with your old friends—and make money, get work experience, or even earn college internship credits. You can apply for jobs at summer camps that specialize in everything from eco-adventure, sports, the arts, or international travel. Being a waterskiing instructor or equestrian counselor, or teaching kids to play soccer in Costa Rica sounds like a lot more fun than working at the mall for three months. (Not that there's anything wrong with working at the mall or anywhere else, but it's good to explore your options and experience something different!)

Try MySummerCamp.com or CampStaff.com for job listings at hundreds of cool camps in the U.S. and abroad.

5. **Cut yourself—and your friends—some slack.** Despite the best of intentions, there will be times when you're incommunicado for one reason or another. Sometimes you'll be too busy or just not feel like calling. The same applies to your old friends. Make an effort to enjoy and appreciate the contact you do have instead of making friends feel guilty for not calling more often. It's much nicer to be greeted with "I'm so happy to hear from you" than "Why haven't you called?" Remember, too, that people and friendships change. Even if you'd stayed in town, you wouldn't have the same relationships with the same people forever . . . and you can be sure that friends you still have over the years are extremely special, genuine friends.

TIP! Before you move, be sure to get contact info for everyone you might want to reach—this includes your favorite teachers, employers, and neighbors. (You'll need references for new jobs and college apps, so keep in touch through occasional e-mails or holiday greetings.)

#10

DO

remember:

this too shall pass

> When you come to the end of your rope,
> tie a knot and hang on.
> *Franklin D. Roosevelt*

The best thing about being new is that it only lasts so long. Pretty soon you won't get that nervous feeling when you walk into the building every morning. You'll start getting phone calls and feel comfortable enough to call new friends. When you've made it through your first week at your new school, you should be proud of yourself. Acknowledge that you've accomplished something, and enjoy knowing things usually get easier from this point forward. And now that you've settled in, please remember to help out the next "new kid" who comes along. You know how she feels—and how a kind word, smile, or invitation to sit with you at lunch can make the difference between a good and not-so-good first day for her.

It was the best of times. It was the worst of times. It was high school.

These years can be some of the trickiest of your whole life, even if you never have to change schools. So much is in flux: your body and emotions, your relationship with your parents, and all the while your academic and work responsibilities keep growing. Add the stress of moving on top of all the other changes, and it's easy to feel overwhelmed. Try your best to keep things in perspective. High school is a mere four years of what will hopefully be a long and interesting journey through life. If you ask enough adults about their high school days, you'd get responses ranging from "It was the best time of my life. I wish I could go back" to "It was a living hell. I counted the days till it was over." Whatever your experience, hang in there and make the best of it.

Bummed Out vs. Depressed: What's the Difference?
Starting at a new school is a big adjustment, and being a little blue, frustrated, or even downright angry during the transition is completely natural. However, if negative or destructive emotions become extreme or don't dissipate over time, it's important to take your feelings seriously, and get help if you need it. You may be suffering from depression if you have the following symptoms for two weeks or more:

- You feel fatigued or lethargic, even when you get enough sleep.
- You're especially irritable or angry, even over small things.
- You lose interest in activities you normally enjoy.
- You're tearful or weepy for no apparent reason.

- You have trouble concentrating, remembering, or making decisions.
- You feel worthless, helpless, or hopeless.
- You have thoughts of harming yourself or others.

Don't resign yourself to months of misery. Feeling better may just be a matter of talking to someone, making lifestyle changes, or, in some cases, taking medication. Talk to your parents or another trusted adult, like a doctor or clergy member. Your school guidance counselor can help you, too, or at least point you in the right direction. (Nobody has to know you're not in the counselor's office discussing your course load.) The important thing is that you talk to someone and start enjoying your life again.

The Headless Prom Queen (My last metaphor—I promise!)
When you have a rotten day at school, whether it's related to being new or not, remember that high school won't last forever. At the end of senior year the status quo will change big time. It's a bit like Washington Irving's *The Legend of Sleepy Hollow*. In this classic tale, the headless horseman appears each Halloween to chop off some unfortunate person's head to replace his own. However— and this is an important detail—the ghost's power ends at the covered bridge from the hollow. Once you cross the bridge, noggin intact, you're home free. Consider graduation your bridge. After school is over, the most popular kids are no longer the center of the universe—

they're just people who you used to go to school with. It's the end of one era and the beginning of another. Sure, your responsibilities will increase, but so will your freedom to make your own decisions and chart your own course. Plus, you'll be better prepared than most kids to make the next big move to college—because once you've survived moving to a new high school, the rest is a piece of cake. (Okay, that is seriously my last metaphor.)